MY CROSS STITCH DOLL

FUN AND EASY PATTERNS FOR OVER 20 CROSS-STITCHED DOLLS

Susan Bates

DAVID & CHARLES

www.davidandcharles.com

JESS   FINN   AMY   BILLIE   TINA

STEVIE   DAISY   MARLA   BOBBIE   VIOLET

MEL   LIZZIE   SASHA   GRACE   HARPER

JAMES   LAYLA   ALFIE   ELLA   RUBY

CONTENTS

INTRODUCTION

Dolls never go out of fashion, despite the introduction of computer games and electronic toys. There's something comforting about having one to cuddle. A doll is a best friend: someone to take with you on an adventure, tell your secrets to and have tea parties with. Part of the fun of having a doll is dressing them, brushing their hair and looking after them – and of course, creating imaginary worlds for you both to inhabit.

As a child, I had quite a few dolls and teddy bears. I had lots of fun dressing them up in different outfits and would play with them for hours. My mum taught me sewing and knitting skills in my youth so, before long, I was making clothes for my dolls and teddies. I also learnt how to sew my own clothes, something which I continue to enjoy doing today.

I used to read my sister's teen magazine, which was filled with illustrations of fashion. I loved copying these drawings and I think it was one of the things that sparked my interest in fashion. This love of fashion, along with my knowledge of how to make clothes, helped me to create the outfits for the dolls in this book. As a dressmaker, I pay attention to design details and style lines. I love textiles and mix various patterns and colours of fabric together to make attractive and appealing outfits – and I've done this here, too, for my cross stitch dolls.

The starting point for designing my dolls was the memory of a cloth doll that I made for myself as a child. It had a large head, a simply constructed body, wool for hair and a cute smiling face. I sketched out something similar for the first doll of this book. Once I'd worked out the main body shape, the fun part began. I really enjoyed creating all of the different hairstyles and clothes for them, seeing them take on a life of their own, each with their own personalities.

My aim with this book was to design a set of dolls that would appeal to grown-ups as well as children. While you may not want to play with them as an adult, you could display them on a shelf as pretty keepsakes, or keep them in your sewing room – if you are lucky enough to have a dedicated sewing space.

This book provides you with the patterns for 20 different dolls, each one in its own unique and colourful outfit. They all come with a front and back panel, which are stitched together and filled with stuffing to make a three-dimensional doll, which I hope you will treasure for years to come.

The designs are made up of full cross stitches, meaning that no tricky fractional stitches are used. There's backstitching in some areas, to add extra details to the clothes and for facial features – but generally you should find them pretty easy to stitch.

The additional heads, torsos and legs charts in the Mix and Match section of the book allow you even more scope to customise parts of the dolls. You could, for example, swap any of the leg sections on the main doll charts with each other or choose one of the extra leg charts, or swap the hair and faces over. This gives you a chance to be imaginative and come up with your own doll outfits and new characters.

This book is a fun way to explore your inner child and to share the joy you discover with the younger people in your life.

Happy stitching!

TOOLS AND MATERIALS

Threads

The designs in this book have been stitched using DMC stranded cotton (floss). These embroidery threads come in a beautiful array of colours and are widely available. Each thread is made up of six strands, from which the required number of strands need to be separated. For stitching onto 28-count evenweave fabric you should stitch with two strands for the full cross stitches and one strand for backstitch. You can use the same number of strands if you choose to stitch onto 14-count Aida fabric. If you find that you want the backstitch to stand out more, you could try stitching with two strands of thread instead of one.

Fabric

Cross stitching is usually done on a fabric that has an even weave, which means that the warp and the weft of the fabric have the same number of threads per inch. The number of threads per inch defines the 'thread count' of that fabric.

The designs in this book are stitched on 28-count evenweave white fabric, which is equivalent to 14-count Aida. Evenweave is worked by stitching over two threads of the weave of the fabric. I would recommend using evenweave fabric rather than Aida as it's a finer weave and is less prone to fraying. This means that it's easier to stitch when you're sewing together the front and back panels of your dolls.

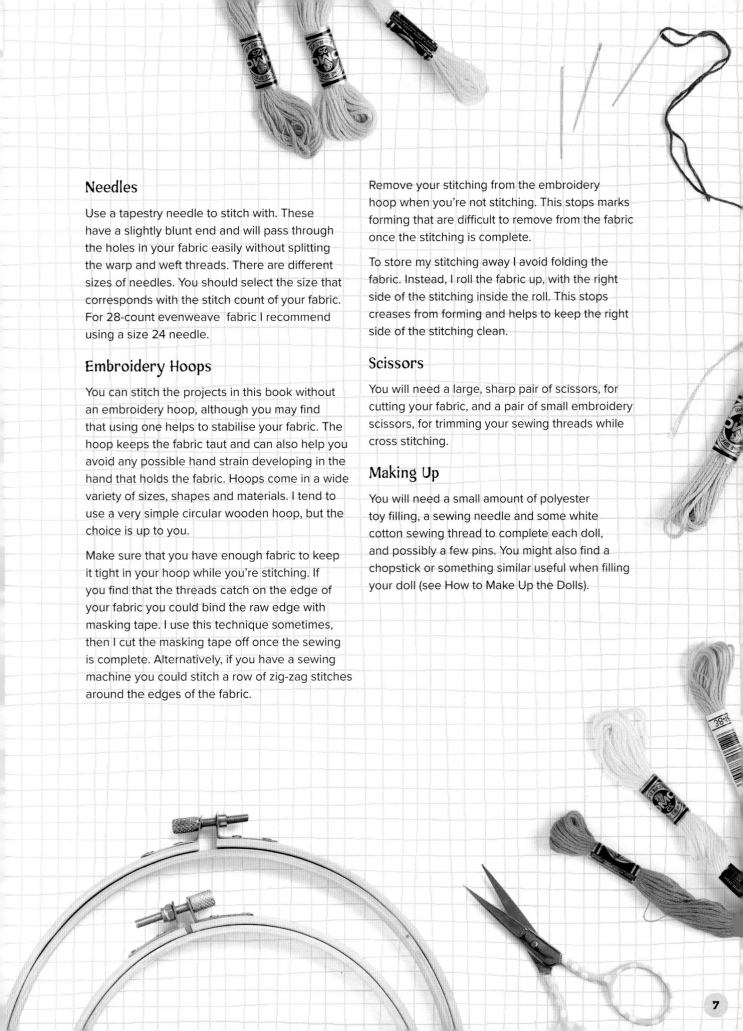

Needles

Use a tapestry needle to stitch with. These have a slightly blunt end and will pass through the holes in your fabric easily without splitting the warp and weft threads. There are different sizes of needles. You should select the size that corresponds with the stitch count of your fabric. For 28-count evenweave fabric I recommend using a size 24 needle.

Embroidery Hoops

You can stitch the projects in this book without an embroidery hoop, although you may find that using one helps to stabilise your fabric. The hoop keeps the fabric taut and can also help you avoid any possible hand strain developing in the hand that holds the fabric. Hoops come in a wide variety of sizes, shapes and materials. I tend to use a very simple circular wooden hoop, but the choice is up to you.

Make sure that you have enough fabric to keep it tight in your hoop while you're stitching. If you find that the threads catch on the edge of your fabric you could bind the raw edge with masking tape. I use this technique sometimes, then I cut the masking tape off once the sewing is complete. Alternatively, if you have a sewing machine you could stitch a row of zig-zag stitches around the edges of the fabric.

Remove your stitching from the embroidery hoop when you're not stitching. This stops marks forming that are difficult to remove from the fabric once the stitching is complete.

To store my stitching away I avoid folding the fabric. Instead, I roll the fabric up, with the right side of the stitching inside the roll. This stops creases from forming and helps to keep the right side of the stitching clean.

Scissors

You will need a large, sharp pair of scissors, for cutting your fabric, and a pair of small embroidery scissors, for trimming your sewing threads while cross stitching.

Making Up

You will need a small amount of polyester toy filling, a sewing needle and some white cotton sewing thread to complete each doll, and possibly a few pins. You might also find a chopstick or something similar useful when filling your doll (see How to Make Up the Dolls).

THE DOLLS

JESS

Hi, I'm Jess. I love sketching and painting, and making my own clothes. I'm drawn to vintage fabrics and like to re-purpose old clothes to 'make them my own'. I may be a creative soul, but I can be practical too – I can put up shelves and do a spot of DIY when needed.

→INFO

Stitch count: (front and back) 62 x 118
Finished size: 11.5 x 21.5cm (4½ x 8½in) when stitched on 28-count evenweave fabric

Model stitched by Sandra Doolan

SHOPPING LIST

→ 1 skein each of DMC stranded cotton thread (floss) as listed in the chart key

→ 2 pieces of 28-count antique white evenweave fabric at least 19 x 29cm (7½ x 11½in) – one piece for the doll front and one for the back

→ Tapestry needle, for cross stitching

→ Pins, for pinning the front and back doll pieces together

→ Sewing needle and thread, for stitching the front and back doll pieces together

→ Polyester toy filling, for stuffing the doll

→ Scissors

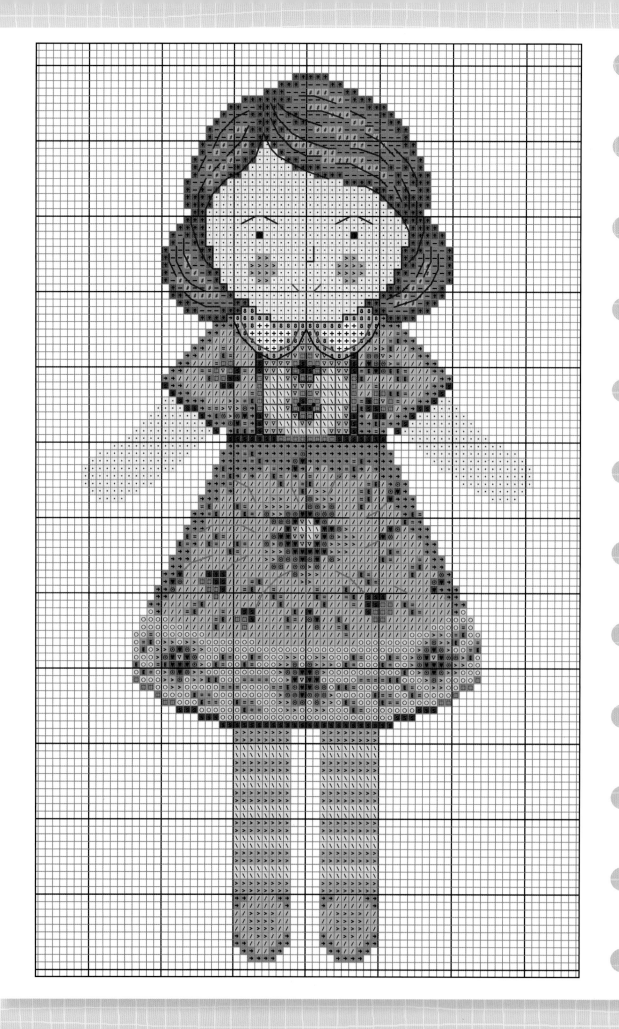

JESS

KEY

Cross stitch

■	938
−	436
✦	809
○	747
+	B5200
\	727
▦	3806
◉	352
∙	3770
=	993
✚	780
#	738
/	3325
8	01
▽	725
⬛	3804
◤	351
>	20
⬛	3814

Backstitch

—	938
—	3814
—	351
—	777

French knot

●	777

13

FINN

Hi, I'm Finn. Here I am in my cosy Fair Isle jumper. I love being outdoors and wear it to keep warm on long walks in the countryside. After my adventures I like to curl up by the fire with a good book and a mug of hot chocolate.

→INFO

Stitch count: (front and back) 62 x 117
Finished size: 11.5 x 21.5cm (4½ x 8½in) when stitched on 28-count evenweave fabric

Model stitched by Sandra Doolan

→ 1 skein each of DMC stranded cotton thread (floss) as listed in the chart key

→ 2 pieces of 28-count antique white evenweave fabric at least 19 x 29cm (7½ x 11½in) – one piece for the doll front and one for the back

→ Tapestry needle, for cross stitching

→ Pins, for pinning the front and back doll pieces together

→ Sewing needle and thread, for stitching the front and back doll pieces together

→ Polyester toy filling, for stuffing the doll

→ Scissors

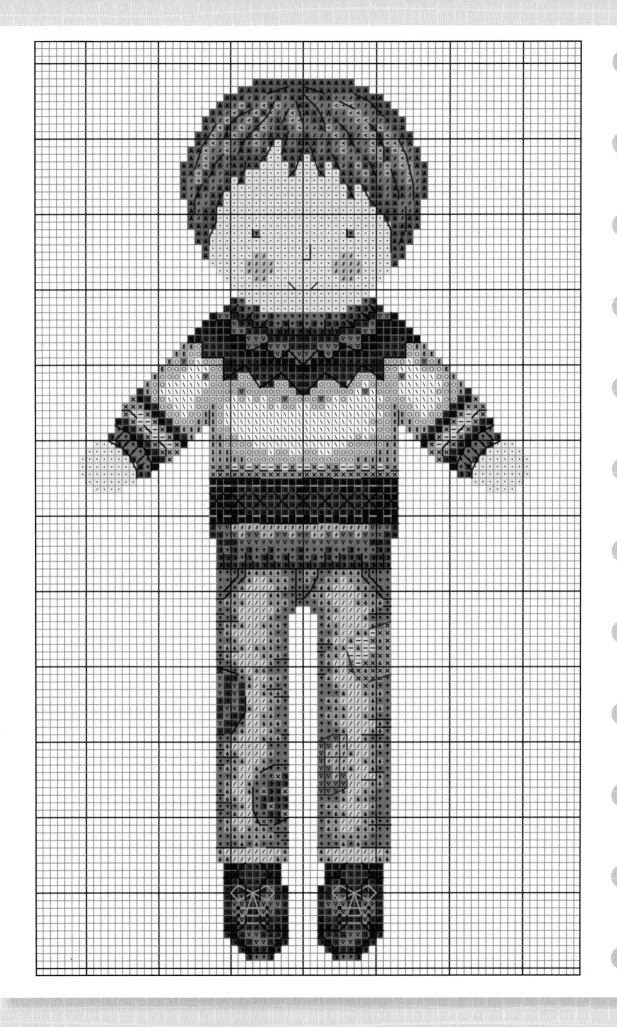

FINN

KEY

Cross stitch

■	321
▽	352
⦂	819
—	744
↑	3810
/	747
O	3033
▲	780
<	738
■	350
#	967
✕	742
■	3808
6	3766
\	Blanc
E	3782
∦	436

Backstitch

-------	742
——	815
——	350
——	823
——	938

French knot

●	823

AMY

Hi, I'm Amy. I'm unashamedly girly. I like pink and sparkles and sequins. I love to dance and dream of one day being a Prima Ballerina! I like being the centre of attention and dressing up for parties. My favourite pet would be a unicorn.

→INFO

Stitch count: (front and back) 62 x 128
Finished size: 11.5 x 23.5cm (4½ x 9¼in) when stitched on 28-count evenweave fabric

Model stitched by Nicola Gravener

→ 1 skein each of DMC stranded cotton thread (floss) as listed in the chart key

→ 2 pieces of 28-count antique white evenweave fabric at least 19 x 32cm (7½ x 12½in) – one piece for the doll front and one for the back

→ Tapestry needle, for cross stitching

→ Pins, for pinning the front and back doll pieces together

→ Sewing needle and thread, for stitching the front and back doll pieces together

→ Polyester toy filling, for stuffing the doll

→ Scissors

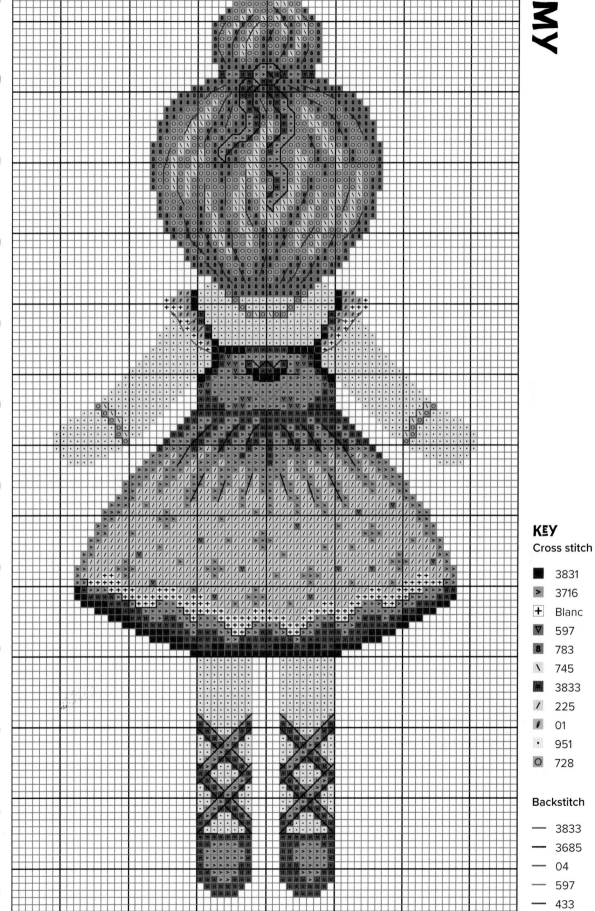

AMY

KEY

Cross stitch

■	3831
>	3716
✛	Blanc
▽	597
8	783
⟍	745
▦	3833
∕	225
#	01
·	951
◉	728

Backstitch

—	3833
—	3685
—	04
—	597
—	433

BILLIE

Hi, I'm Billie. Summer is my best time of year. I love to be at the seaside, building sandcastles and searching for pretty coloured shells on the beach. When the tide goes out I have fun looking at tiny creatures in the rock pools. My favourite ice cream flavour is strawberry.

→INFO

Stitch count: (front and back) 60 x 119
Finished size: 11 x 21.5cm (4¼ x 8½in) when stitched on 28-count evenweave fabric

Model stitched by Sandra Doolan

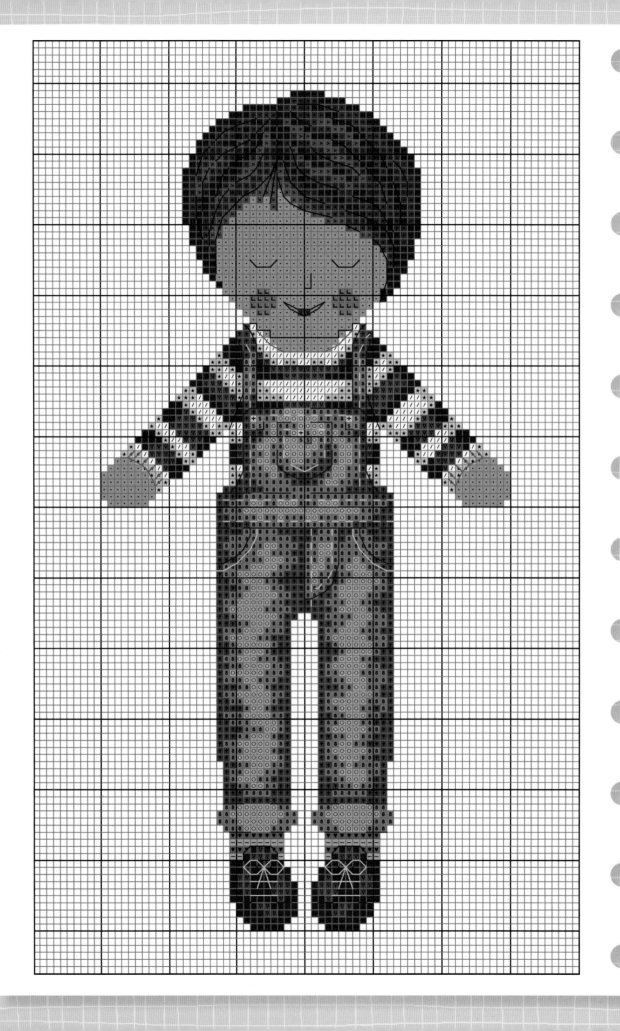

BILLIE

KEY

Cross stitch

●	3864
■	301
■	349
⊔	352
⁄	B5200
+	726
8	813
♥	911
■	300
▷	976
▽	351
★	01
s	3820
✦	517
○	162
−	954

Backstitch

—	3371
—	815
—	414
—	726
—	311

TINA

Hi, I'm Valentina (or Tina for short), and I love pretty flowers. The dahlia is my favourite, with its large colourful blooms. I'm not sure which shade I like best as I love them all! I enjoy spending time in the forest, listening to the calls of all the amazing birds and animals.

→INFO

Stitch count: (front and back) 64 x 129

Finished size: 11.5 x 23.5cm (4½ x 9¼in) when stitched on 28-count evenweave fabric

Model stitched by Emma Rhodes

SHOPPING LIST

→ 1 skein each of DMC stranded cotton thread (floss) as listed in the chart key

→ 2 pieces of 28-count antique white evenweave fabric at least 19 x 31cm (7½ x 12¼in) – one piece for the doll front and one for the back

→ Tapestry needle, for cross stitching

→ Pins, for pinning the front and back doll pieces together

→ Sewing needle and thread, for stitching the front and back doll pieces together

→ Polyester toy filling, for stuffing the doll

→ Scissors

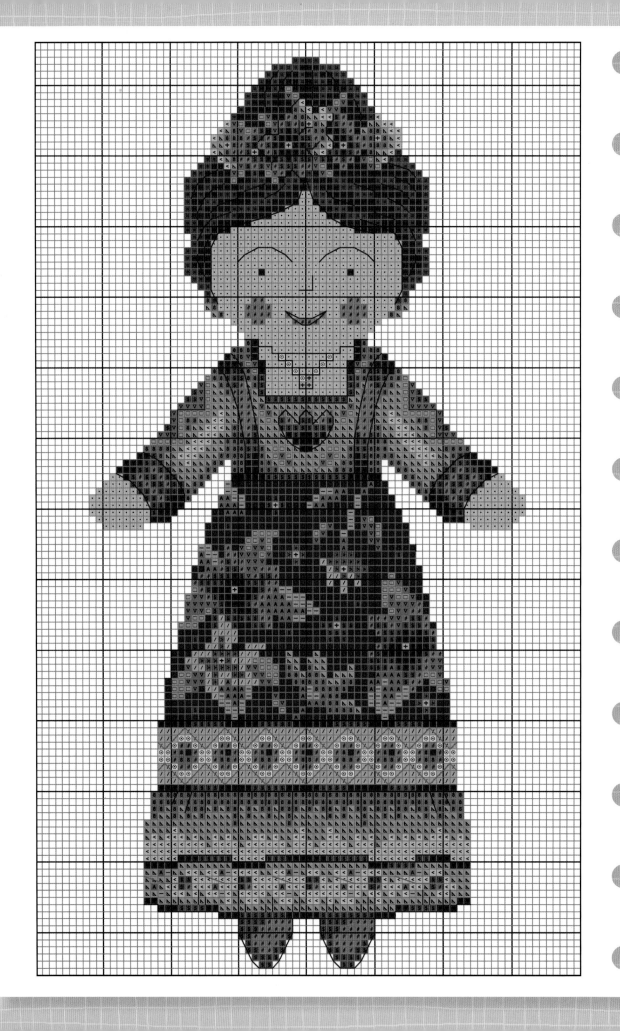

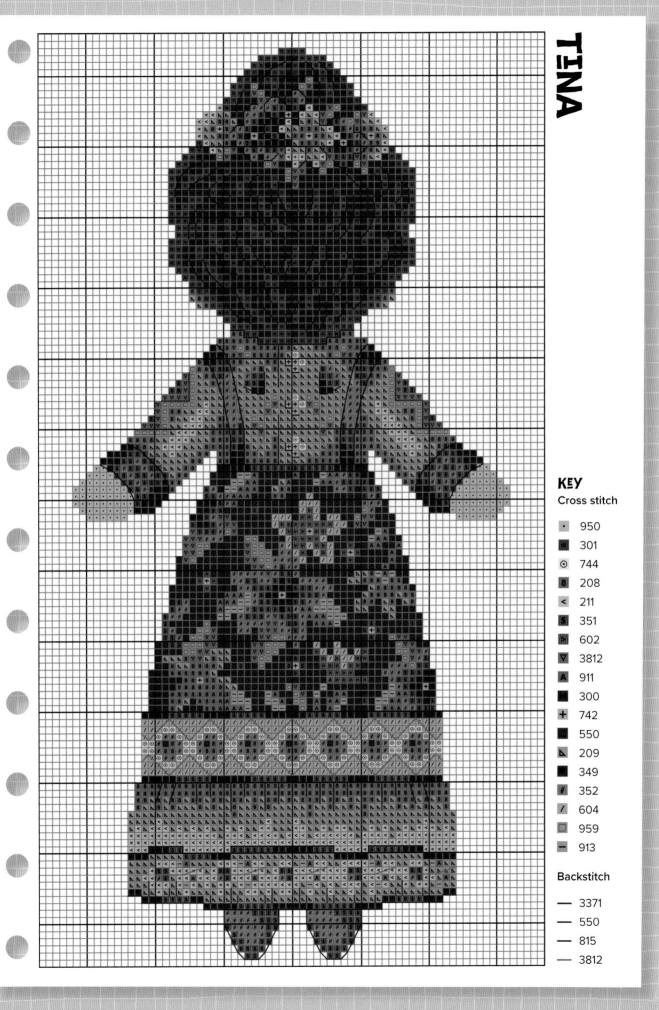

KEY

Cross stitch

·	950
▦	301
⊙	744
8	208
<	211
s	351
⋈	602
▽	3812
A	911
■	300
+	742
■	550
◣	209
■	349
#	352
/	604
□	959
–	913

Backstitch

—	3371
—	550
—	815
—	3812

STEVIE

Hi, I'm Stevie. I'm all wrapped up in the hat, scarf and mittens that my grandma knitted for me. The countryside looks so pretty with a covering of white snow that I just had to get out there! Making a snowman is one of my favourite things to do in the winter.

→INFO

Stitch count: (front and back) 62 x 124

Finished size: 11.5 x 22.5cm (4½ x 8⅞in) when stitched on 28-count evenweave fabric

Model stitched by Eleanor Cooper

➜ 1 skein each of DMC stranded cotton thread (floss) as listed in the chart key

➜ 2 pieces of 28-count antique white evenweave fabric at least 19 x 30.5cm (7½ x 12in) – one piece for the doll front and one for the back

➜ Tapestry needle, for cross stitching

➜ Pins, for pinning the front and back doll pieces together

➜ Sewing needle and thread, for stitching the front and back doll pieces together

➜ Polyester toy filling, for stuffing the doll

➜ Scissors

KEY

Cross stitch

⠋	3774
■	3801
6	761
E	01
▯	798
♥	3848
⊟	3811
◣	435
◉	931
■	321
✖	3833
/	225
⊙	B5200
S	809
✦	959
■	434
■	930
◥	932

Backstitch

—	898
—	815
⚌	B5200
—	04
—	3808
—	3848

DAISY

Hi, I'm Daisy. I love spending time in my garden. Sunflowers are my favourite flower – with their huge bright heads that turn towards the sun. Gardening really relaxes me, and my garden is my happy place!

→INFº

Stitch count: (front and back) 62 x 116
Finished size: 11.5 x 21cm (4½ x 8¼in) when stitched on 28-count evenweave fabric

Model stitched by Nicola Gravener

SHOPPING LIST

→ 1 skein each of DMC stranded cotton thread (floss) as listed in the chart key

→ 2 pieces of 28-count antique white evenweave fabric at least 19 x 29cm (7½ x 11½in) – one piece for the doll front and one for the back

→ Tapestry needle, for cross stitching

→ Pins, for pinning the front and back doll pieces together

→ Sewing needle and thread, for stitching the front and back doll pieces together

→ Polyester toy filling, for stuffing the doll

→ Scissors

DAISY

KEY

Cross stitch

S	976
░	3770
◣	352
O	725
▽	Blanc
∦	703
=	3810
\	747
+	3827
✚	351
−	20
/	727
★	701
>	16
6	3766

Backstitch

—	975
—	321
—	351
—	976
—	890
—	3808

French knot

●	976

MARLA

Hi, I'm Marla. My most beloved hobbies are reading, playing board games with my friends, and doing fun science experiments. My favourite food, if I had to choose just one, would be blueberry jam sandwiches.

→INFº

Stitch count: (front and back) 62 x 118

Finished size: 11.5 x 21.5cm (4½ x 8½in) when stitched on 28-count evenweave fabric

Model stitched by Madeleine Ayme-McLean

→ 1 skein each of DMC stranded cotton thread (floss) as listed in the chart key

→ 2 pieces of 28-count antique white evenweave fabric at least 19 x 29cm (7½ x 11½in) – one piece for the doll front and one for the back

→ Tapestry needle, for cross stitching

→ Pins, for pinning the front and back doll pieces together

→ Sewing needle and thread, for stitching the front and back doll pieces together

→ Polyester toy filling, for stuffing the doll

→ Scissors

KEY

Cross stitch

■	938
▦	3772
>	209
■	917
◉	807
■	321
▥	351
=	3713
■	433
✳	208
−	26
▨	3607
▽	3766
▤	349
+	3851
/	819

Backstitch

—	310
—	728
—	550
—	3808
—	815
—	3851
—	3607

BOBBIE

Hi, I'm Bobbie. I'm happiest wearing my vintage baseball jacket and jeans. My favourite food is hot dogs with mustard, and I like to snack on salted caramel popcorn while chilling out and watching a good movie.

→INFO

Stitch count: (front and back) 58 x 118
Finished size: 11 x 21.5cm (4¼ x 8½in) when stitched on 28-count evenweave fabric

Model stitched by Madeleine Ayme-McLean

SHOPPING LIST

→ 1 skein each of DMC stranded cotton thread (floss) as listed in the chart key

→ 2 pieces of 28-count antique white evenweave fabric at least 18.5 x 29cm (7¼ x 11½in) – one piece for the doll front and one for the back

→ Tapestry needle, for cross stitching

→ Pins, for pinning the front and back doll pieces together

→ Sewing needle and thread, for stitching the front and back doll pieces together

→ Polyester toy filling, for stuffing the doll

→ Scissors

BOBBIE

KEY

Cross stitch

Symbol	Code
·	3864
■	801
N	436
/	606
>	725
<	792
★	910
S	760
V	434
■	817
⊙	741
#	727
O	793
▬	912
↟	720

Backstitch

	Code
—	3371
—	817
—	815
—	823
—	157
—	3818

VIOLET

Hi, I'm Violet. I love music and I sing in a band with my friends. I also play guitar. I love pretty dresses and stripey clothes, and my favourite colour is purple, so much so that I've even dyed my hair purple!

→**INFO**

Stitch count: (front and back) 62 x 118
Finished size: 11.5 x 21.5cm (4½ x 8½in) when stitched on 28-count evenweave fabric

Model stitched by Emma Rhodes

➜ 1 skein each of DMC stranded cotton thread (floss) as listed in the chart key

➜ 2 pieces of 28-count antique white evenweave fabric at least 19 x 29cm (7½ x 11½in) – one piece for the doll front and one for the back

➜ Tapestry needle, for cross stitching

➜ Pins, for pinning the front and back doll pieces together

➜ Sewing needle and thread, for stitching the front and back doll pieces together

➜ Polyester toy filling, for stuffing the doll

➜ Scissors

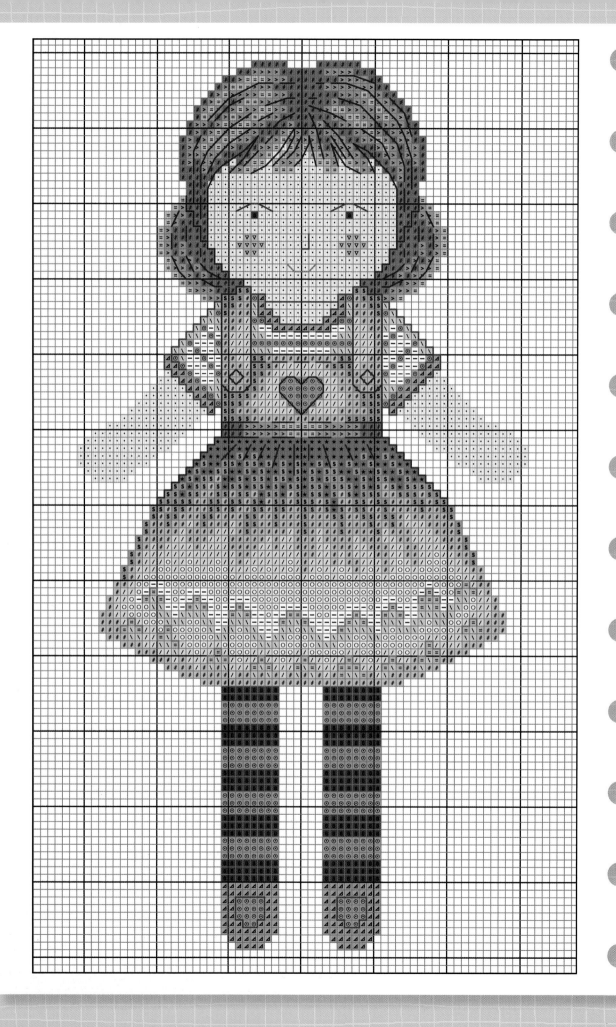

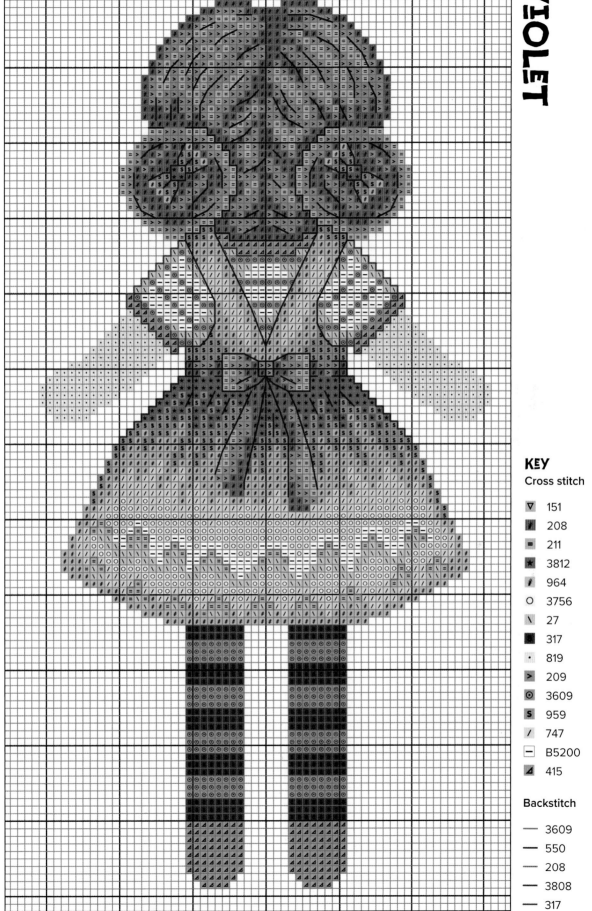

VIOLET

KEY
Cross stitch

▽	151
▦	208
=	211
★	3812
#	964
○	3756
\	27
■	317
⦂	819
>	209
◉	3609
S	959
/	747
−	B5200
◢	415

Backstitch

—	3609
—	550
—	208
—	3808
—	317

MEL

Hi, I'm Mel. I'm really into sport, especially soccer. At weekends you'll find me playing for my local team. I'm a striker – I love scoring goals. When I'm not playing soccer I'll be watching it on TV. I enjoy exercise and I have lots of energy!

→INFº

Stitch count: (front and back) 60 x 122
Finished size: 11.5 x 22cm (4½ x 8¾in) when stitched on 28-count evenweave fabric

Model stitched by Nicola Gravener

→ 1 skein each of DMC stranded cotton thread (floss) as listed in the chart key

→ 2 pieces of 28-count antique white evenweave fabric at least 19 x 30.5cm (7½ x 12in) – one piece for the doll front and one for the back

→ Tapestry needle, for cross stitching

→ Pins, for pinning the front and back doll pieces together

→ Sewing needle and thread, for stitching the front and back doll pieces together

→ Polyester toy filling, for stuffing the doll

→ Scissors

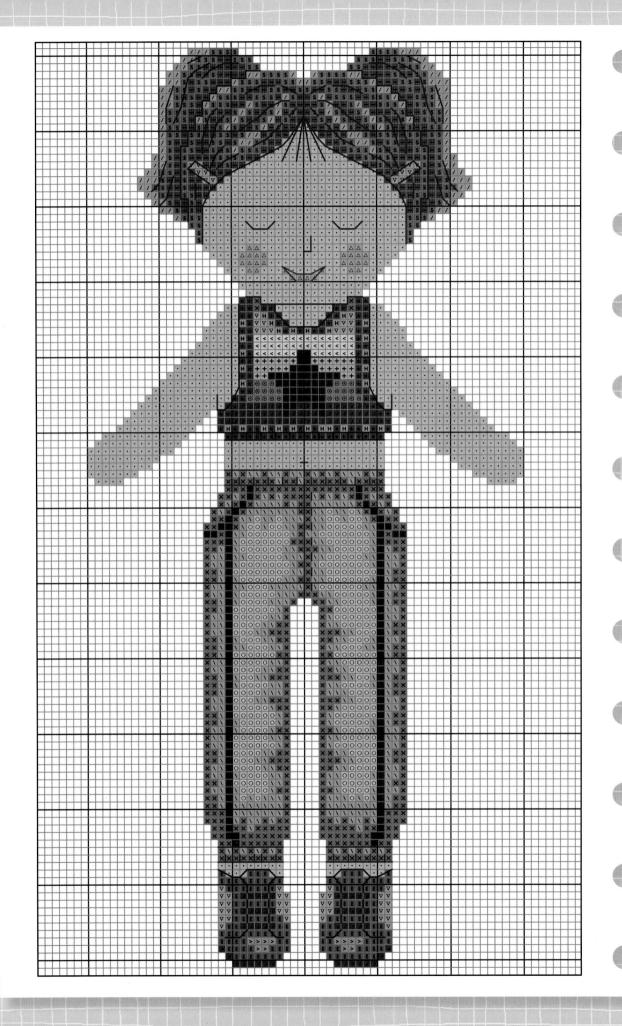

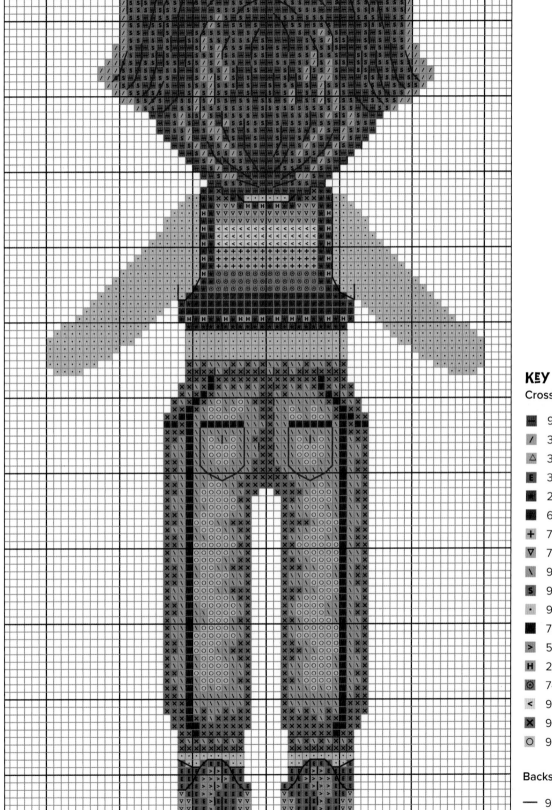

KEY

Cross stitch

▨	975
╱	3827
△	3326
E	3760
▨	208
▨	666
+	742
▽	704
╲	959
S	976
·	950
■	797
▶	519
H	210
◉	740
◂	973
✕	943
○	964

Backstitch

—	938
—	666
—	797
—	3808

LIZZIE

Hi, I'm Lizzie. I'm a city girl at heart. I love to shop at the weekend and meet my friends for coffee, cake and a chat. We have so much fun catching up – we often lose track of time and could talk for hours!

→INFO

Stitch count: (front and back) 60 x 116
Finished size: 11.5 x 21cm (4½ x 8¼in) when stitched on 28-count evenweave fabric

Model stitched by Eleanor Cooper

SHOPPING LIST

→ 1 skein each of DMC stranded cotton thread (floss) as listed in the chart key

→ 2 pieces of 28-count antique white evenweave fabric at least 19 x 29cm (7½ x 11½in) – one piece for the doll front and one for the back

→ Tapestry needle, for cross stitching

→ Pins, for pinning the front and back doll pieces together

→ Sewing needle and thread, for stitching the front and back doll pieces together

→ Polyester toy filling, for stuffing the doll

→ Scissors

LIZZIE

KEY

Cross stitch

8	782
−	3822
T	322
O	800
A	603
#	992
\	3811
>	3820
⫶	948
=	813
✳	601
/	605
S	3766

Backstitch

—	601
—	801
—	796
—	498
—	991

SASHA

Hi, I'm Sasha. I like to read,
especially books about animals.
I volunteer at a local animal
shelter and have been known
to take a rescue animal home.
I have lots of cats and dogs
and my favourite new pet is an
iguana called Ozzie.

→INFO

Stitch count: (front and back) 62 x 116

Finished size: 11.5 x 21cm (4½ x 8¼in)
when stitched on 28-count evenweave
fabric

Model stitched by Sandra Doolan

→ 1 skein each of DMC stranded cotton thread (floss) as listed in the chart key

→ 2 pieces of 28-count antique white evenweave fabric at least 19 x 29cm (7½ x 11½in) – one piece for the doll front and one for the back

→ Tapestry needle, for cross stitching

→ Pins, for pinning the front and back doll pieces together

→ Sewing needle and thread, for stitching the front and back doll pieces together

→ Polyester toy filling, for stuffing the doll

→ Scissors

SASHA

KEY

Cross stitch

▨	433
▪	3864
＼	3824
■	817
◉	3706
／	3326
#	712
◉	783
▤	435
▽	3340
+	728
◣	3705
＜	961
▨	3607
8	Blanc
＞	676

Backstitch

—	3340
—	817
—	3371
—	777

GRACE

Hi, I'm Grace. My granny knitted this stripey jumper for me – I love it and I wear it all the time! In my rucksack I have my art supplies for some outdoor sketching, plus some of Granny's chocolate chip cookies for a quick snack.

→INFO

Stitch count: (front and back) 62 x 126
Finished size: 11.5 x 23cm (4½ x 9in) when stitched on 28-count evenweave fabric

Model stitched by Eleanor Cooper

GRACE

KEY

Cross stitch

■	400
·	948
✚	334
6	775
▥	351
≠	761
<	712
=	3846
◫	3776
◨	825
>	3325
■	349
▽	760
◑	822
/	Blanc
◣	3844
★	726

Backstitch

—	938
⋯	726
—	336
—	349
—	498

HARPER

Hi, I'm Harper. In the evenings I like to relax in a lavender scented bubble bath. Afterwards, I put on my warm and cosy pyjamas, get into bed and snuggle up with my favourite teddy bear, Honey.

→INFO

Stitch count: (front and back) 60 x 117
Finished size: 11.5 x 21.5cm (4½ x 8½in) when stitched on 28-count evenweave fabric

Model stitched by Emma Rhodes

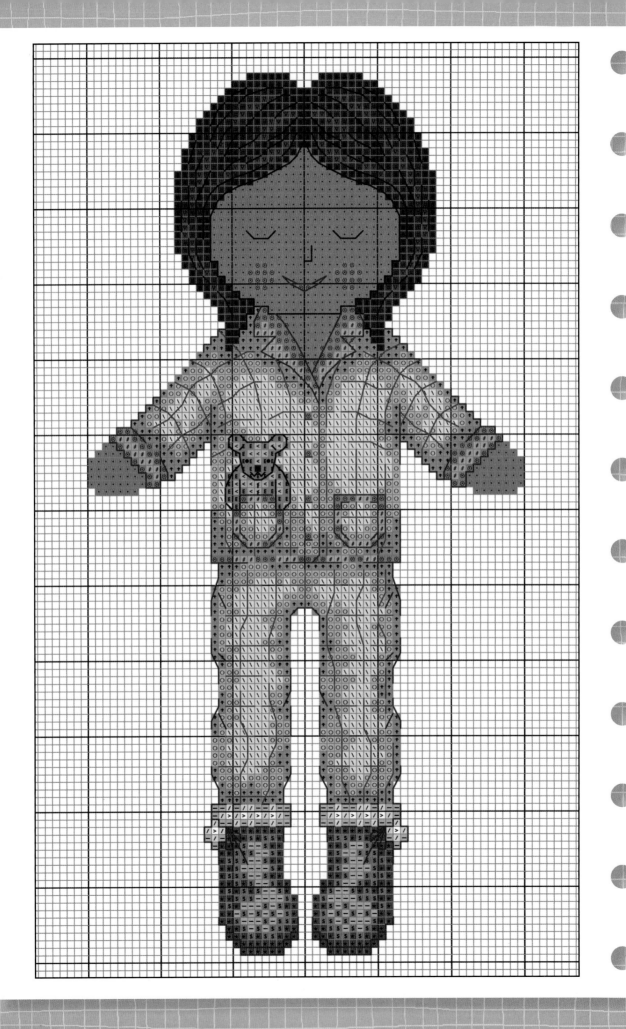

KEY

Cross stitch

■	898
W	301
◎	899
↑	807
\	747
/	24
S	209
E	435
■	310
■	400
■	3772
#	3326
O	3766
>	B5200
−	153
■	208
<	437

Backstitch

—	310
—	326
—	3842
—	550
—	208

French knot

●	310

JAMES

Hi, I'm James. I'm a keen writer of short stories. My greatest wish is to be a best-selling author. I'm also crazy about art, and my favourite artist is Vincent van Gogh.

→INFO

Stitch count: (front and back) 62 x 118
Finished size: 11.5 x 21.5cm (4½ x 8½in) when stitched on 28-count evenweave fabric

Model stitched by Sandra Doolan

SHOPPING LIST

→ 1 skein each of DMC stranded cotton thread (floss) as listed in the chart key

→ 2 pieces of 28-count antique white evenweave fabric at least 19 x 29cm (7½ x 11½in) – one piece for the doll front and one for the back

→ Tapestry needle, for cross stitching

→ Pins, for pinning the front and back doll pieces together

→ Sewing needle and thread, for stitching the front and back doll pieces together

→ Polyester toy filling, for stuffing the doll

→ Scissors

KEY

Cross stitch

⊙	725
S	434
\	151
◣	987
E	645
O	3024
/	Blanc
H	3687
■	938
▬	436
·	951
+	989
<	3023
=	712
▽	3688
■	154

Backstitch

—	938
⋯	725
—	721
—	890
—	3799
—	3687
—	154

LAYLA

Hi, I'm Layla. I'm at my happiest riding my pony, Beauty. I take her on long trail rides through the forests where I live. She's a gorgeous chestnut colour, with a long, golden mane and tail that I love to brush and plait.

→INFO

Stitch count: (front and back) 62 x 122

Finished size: 11.5 x 22cm (4½ x 8¾in) when stitched on 28-count evenweave fabric

Model stitched by Caroline Grayling

→ 1 skein each of DMC stranded cotton thread (floss) as listed in the chart key

→ 2 pieces of 28-count antique white evenweave fabric at least 19 x 30.5cm (7½ x 12in) – one piece for the doll front and one for the back

→ Tapestry needle, for cross stitching

→ Pins, for pinning the front and back doll pieces together

→ Sewing needle and thread, for stitching the front and back doll pieces together

→ Polyester toy filling, for stuffing the doll

→ Scissors

KEY

Cross stitch

■	838
◉	3828
·	948
▽	3852
□	744
◯	799
★	910
<	954
▬	606
\	3341
▼	869
=	422
≈	353
+	3821
8	798
/	3325
∦	912
■	817
6	3340

Backstitch

—	838
—	796
—	910
—	14
—	817
—	3821

ALFIE

- - - - - - -

Hi, I'm Alfie. This is the best moment of my life because I'm marrying my sweetheart today! All our friends and family are going to help us celebrate our magical day.

→INFO

Stitch count: (front and back) 62 x 119
Finished size: 11.5 x 21.5cm (4½ x 8½in) when stitched on 28-count evenweave fabric

Model stitched by Caroline Grayling

SHOPPING LIST

→ 1 skein each of DMC stranded cotton thread (floss) as listed in the chart key

→ 2 pieces of 28-count antique white evenweave fabric at least 19 x 29cm (7½ x 11½in) – one piece for the doll front and one for the back

→ Tapestry needle, for cross stitching

→ Pins, for pinning the front and back doll pieces together

→ Sewing needle and thread, for stitching the front and back doll pieces together

→ Polyester toy filling, for stuffing the doll

→ Scissors

ALFIE

KEY

Cross stitch

■	310
◉	317
▽	415
s	Ecru
■	838
▥	435
◎	899
■	3799
=	318
∕	762
+	B5200
■	433
·	407
<	3326

Backstitch

—	310
═	B5200
—	958
—	326

ELLA

Hi, I'm Ella. It's my big day and I'm so excited! I'm marrying the love of my life. We're going to Paris, the city of romance, for our honeymoon.

→INFO

Stitch count: (front and back) 60 x 119

Finished size: 11.5 x 21.5cm (4½ x 8½in) when stitched on 28-count evenweave fabric

Model stitched by Caroline Grayling

SHOPPING LIST

→ 1 skein each of DMC stranded cotton thread (floss) as listed in the chart key

→ 2 pieces of 28-count antique white evenweave fabric at least 18.5 x 29cm (7¼ x 11½in) – one piece for the doll front and one for the back

→ Tapestry needle, for cross stitching

→ Pins, for pinning the front and back doll pieces together

→ Sewing needle and thread, for stitching the front and back doll pieces together

→ Polyester toy filling, for stuffing the doll

→ Scissors

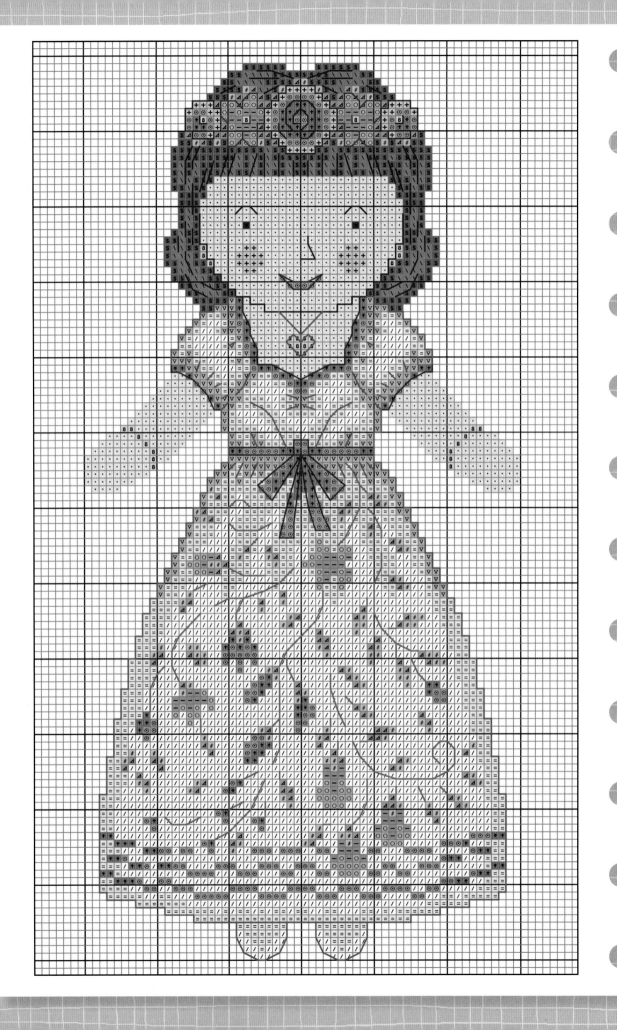

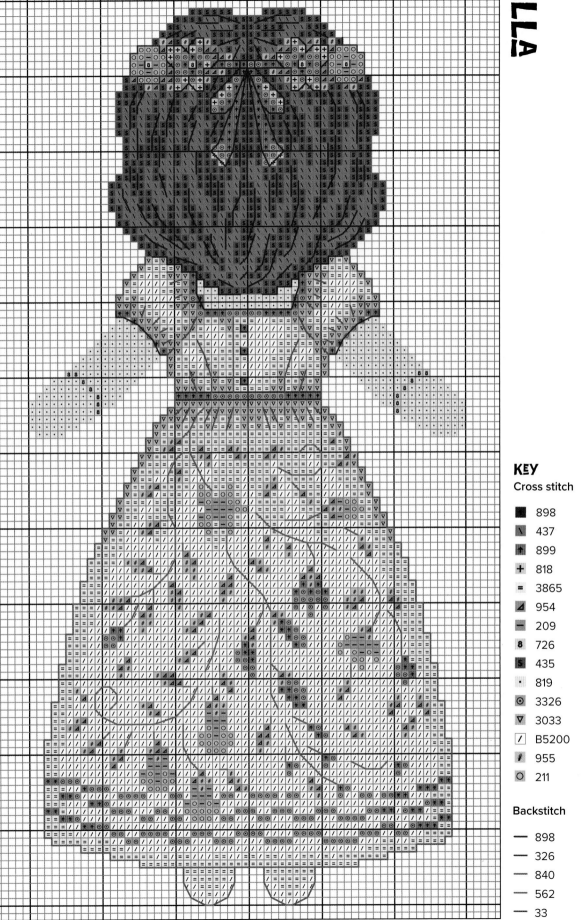

KEY

Cross stitch

■	898
\	437
⊞	899
+	818
=	3865
◸	954
−	209
8	726
⊠	435
·	819
⊙	3326
▽	3033
/	B5200
#	955
◯	211

Backstitch

—	898
—	326
—	840
—	562
—	33

RUBY

Hi, I'm Ruby. I adore birds of paradise – I see them as the most elegant and colourful birds in the world. One of my favourite things to do is to watch them take flight in the beautiful, big blue sky.

→INFO

Stitch count: (front and back) 62 x 119
Finished size: 11.5 x 21.5cm (4½ x 8½in) when stitched on 28-count evenweave fabric

Model stitched by Madeleine Ayme-McLean

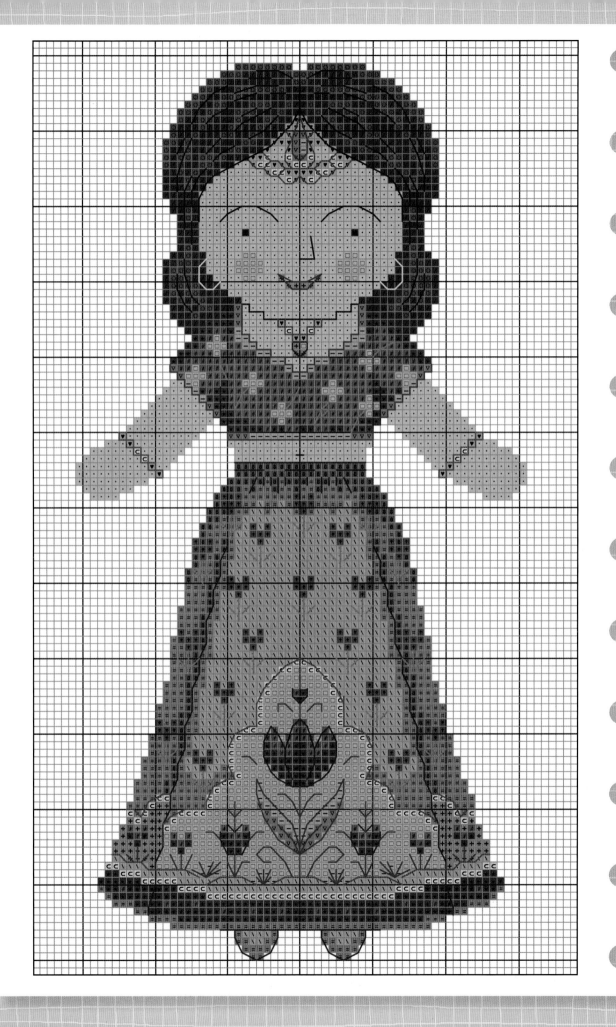

KEY

Cross stitch

■	3371
◑	433
■	321
✶	208
⊟	3340
▽	3814
✛	899
♥	3820
■	938
·	3771
✷	606
8	720
\	3341
▬	993
☐	3326
C	3822

Backstitch

—	321
—	3371
—	814
—	3847
—	3814
—	433
—	3822

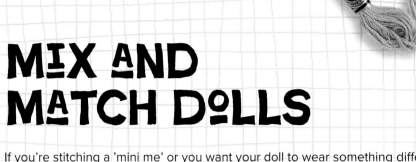

MIX AND MATCH DOLLS

If you're stitching a 'mini me' or you want your doll to wear something different, feel free to mix and match hairstyles and faces, or tops and bottoms, to your heart's content. You can combine any parts from the previous charts, or choose some of the extra elements from this section.

KEY

Cross stitch

■ 801	▽ 01	◪ 3820	◨ 349	◑ 943
◣ 436	✚ 334	▢ 945	6 415	◨ 3829
O 761	▦ 976	▤ 434	− Blanc	< 3822
■ 321	U 3608	> 760	▨ 301	
▨ 351	H 959	▪ 948	▼ 3607	

Backstitch
— 349
— 3371
— 718
— 3847

French knot
● 3371

KEY

Cross stitch

·	948	—	954	■	350	=	3822
○	3864	<	01	S	435		
⌗	352	A	3820	E	912		
■	433	/	819	8	415		
>	437	6	353	\	Blanc		

Backstitch

— 3371
— 898
— 350

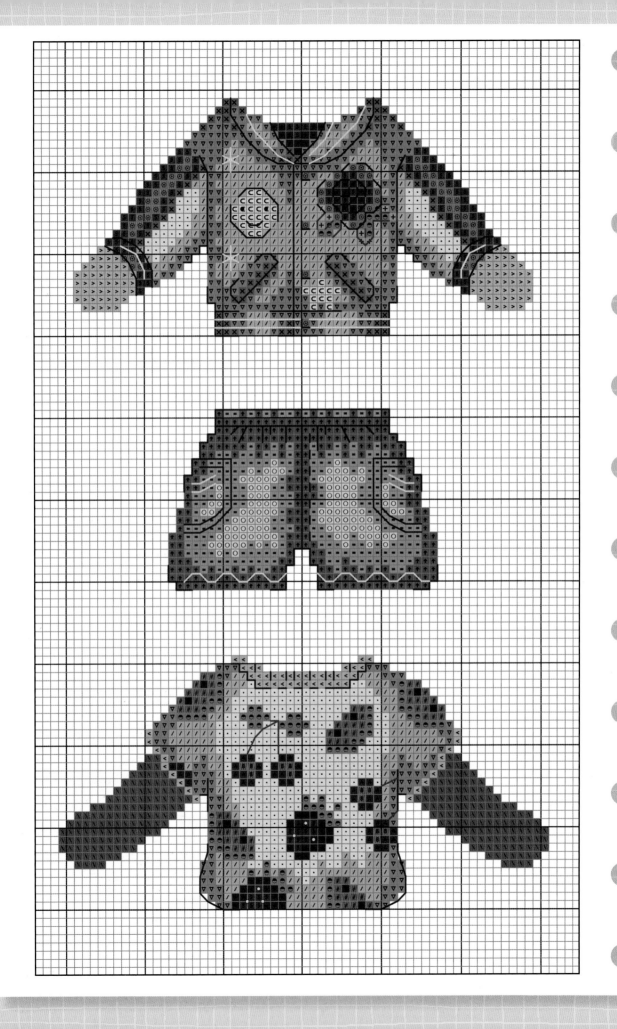

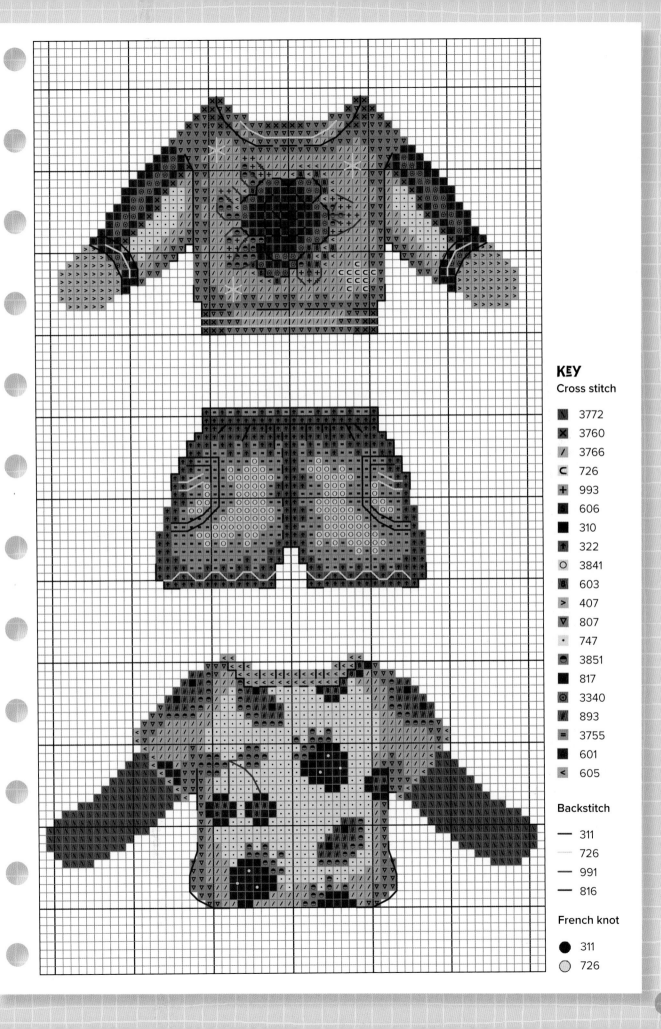

KEY

Cross stitch

◨	3772
✕	3760
╱	3766
C	726
+	993
■	606
■	310
⬆	322
○	3841
▨	603
>	407
▽	807
·	747
◙	3851
■	817
◉	3340
▧	893
=	3755
■	601
<	605

Backstitch

—	311
—	726
—	991
—	816

French knot

●	311
○	726

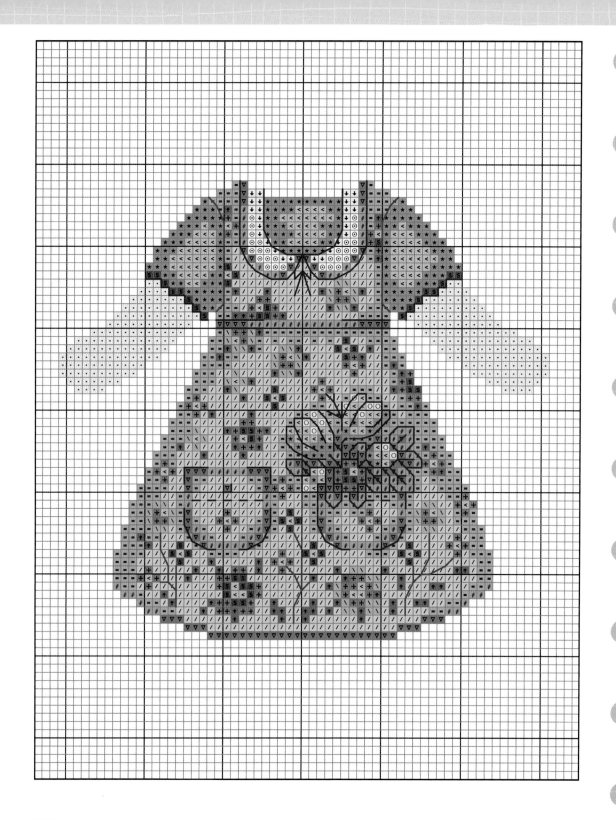

KEY

Cross stitch

- · 3770
- = 3348
- ▽ 597
- ↓ 3756
- ◪ 350
- ◥ 353
- < 3822
- ⬆ 3347
- / 772
- ⋕ 598
- ⊙ B5200
- ✚ 352
- ★ 3820
- ○ 3078

Backstitch

- — 3347
- — 3809
- — 355

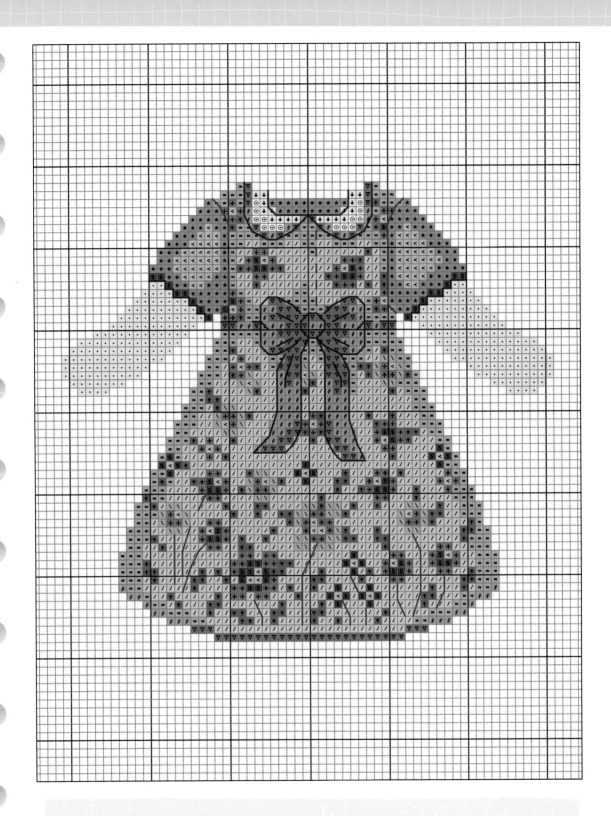

MIX AND MATCH TIP

If you're mixing things up you are obviously going to need to decide at what point to join one design to the other. With heads you can switch to a different upper body at the neckline of the clothing. Just continue the skin tone of the face at the neck where necessary, and for the arms and hands. With trousers and skirts you'll need to change over at the waistband, using your judgment if the waistline is higher on one design than the next. Don't forget to match the skin tone of the legs to the face, if you're choosing shorts or a short skirt.

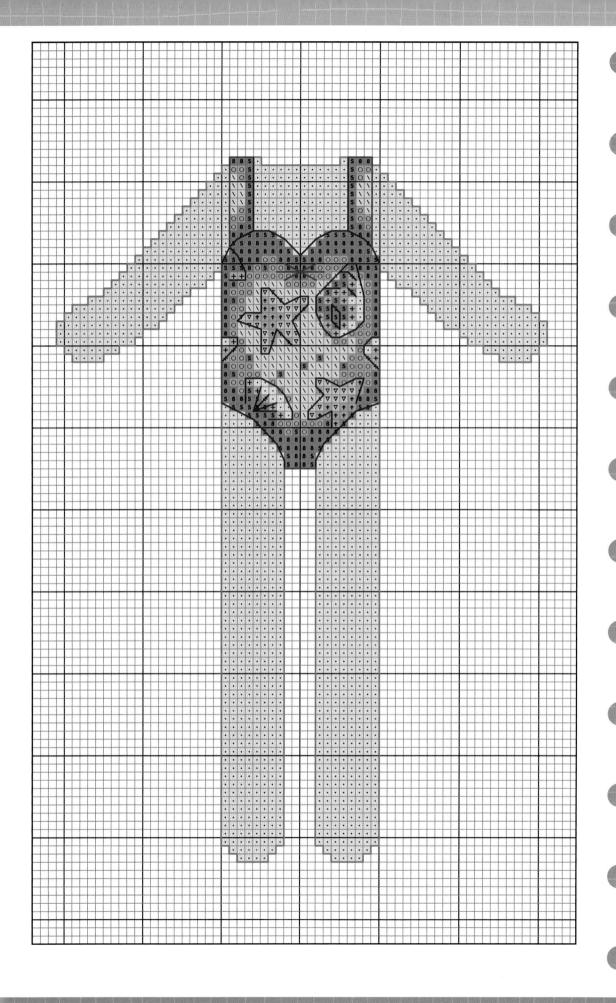

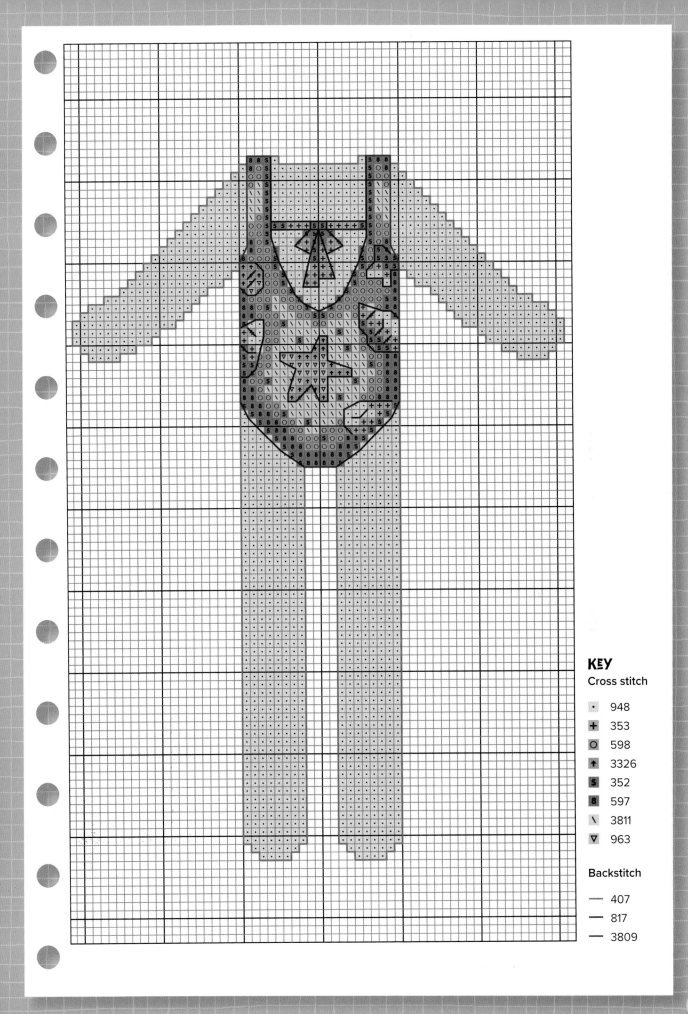

KEY

Cross stitch

⋅	948
+	353
O	598
↑	3326
S	352
8	597
\	3811
▽	963

Backstitch

—	407
—	817
—	3809

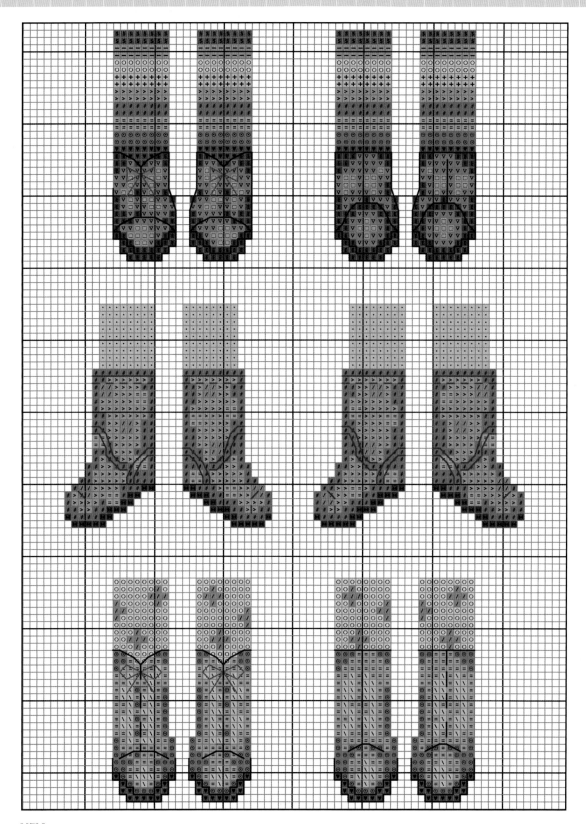

KEY

Cross stitch

- · 948
- ◼ 890
- ▷ 703
- ○ 726
- ⑤ 608
- ▽ 414
- ▼ 3765
- ═ 3846
- ∥ 760
- ⧣ 701
- ╋ 15
- ▬ 741
- ▣ 413
- ▢ 415
- ⊙ 3844
- ⟍ 3766

Backstitch

- —— 608
- —— 890
- —— 310

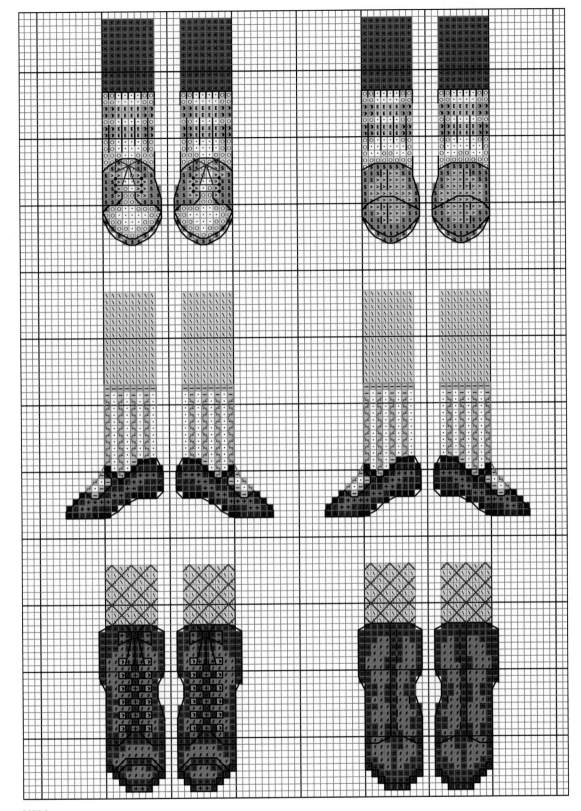

KEY

Cross stitch

◀ 3772	▨ 350	s 912	
▦ 413	◑ 972	■ 817	
— 01	\ 948	✚ 3340	
· Blanc	⌗ 414	E 726	
▷ 954	O Ecru		

Backstitch

— 310
— 414
— 350
— 815

French knot

● 310

TECHNIQUES

In the following pages I've gathered together all the information you will need to cross stitch your doll and then turn it into a little three-dimensional person, ready for adventures or just for admiring. Take a look at the advice on threads and fabric (see Tools and Materials) at the beginning of this book – then away you go!

HOW TO PREPARE

Begin by cutting your fabric to the correct size for the design. For each doll I've specified a suggested size of fabric that you'll need, so cut one piece that size for the front of the doll and one for the back. You need to make sure that you allow an area of unstitched fabric around each of the stitched areas, so that you can put the fabric in a hoop while stitching and have some margin of fabric around the doll design to make it easy when it comes to stitching the front and back pieces together (see How to Make Up the Dolls).

Cut the stranded cotton thread into lengths that are easy to manage, approximately 50cm (20in), or the length of your forearm. Avoid using very long lengths of thread as this can make them prone to tangle. Separate two of the six strands (see Tools and Materials) and use these to stitch with. Keep the other four strands to one side and separate them out into two lots of two strands, for further stitching – or use one strand for backstitching.

Start stitching by working from the centre of the fabric outwards. To do this, find the centre of your fabric by folding it in half widthways and lengthways. Mark the centre of the fabric in a way of your choosing. I sometimes use regular sewing thread to tack a horizontal and then a vertical line of stitches, kind of like a crosshair, in the centre of my fabric. Once I've worked a few cross stitches in the centre I then remove the tacking.

Refer to the chart to find the centre of the design on the pattern and then start stitching from here. If you do this you are making sure that your stitching will fit nicely on the fabric.

The easiest way to start stitching is to hold a small 'tail' of the thread at the back of your work and stitch over it as you go (see How to Cross Stitch). An alternative is to make a knot in the thread, putting the knot on the front of the work and stitch over the thread that forms at the back of the work. When your stitching gets close to the knot you can snip it off. You can use whichever method you prefer – I tend to use the first method mostly.

TOP TIPS FOR TIDY SEWING

• Finish the threads by running them under a few stitches on the back of your stitching. Snip any 'tails' to keep the stitching neat.

• Complete all the full cross stitches first. Then add the backstitching. This adds detail and definition to the design – I've used it on the doll designs as decoration on the clothing and also on the doll's facial features.

• Aim to keep your stitching as neat and tidy as possible. You can run colours from one part of your stitching to another along the back, but don't do this over large areas, as it can affect the tension of your final stitching and make it very messy.

• Always wash your hands before you start sewing. This will keep your work nice and clean.

HOW TO CROSS STITCH

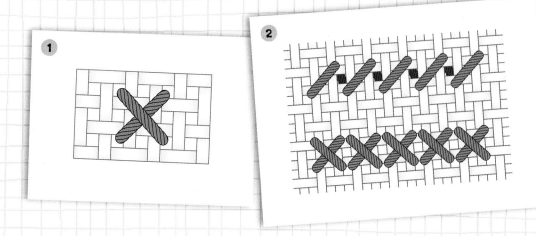

Cross Stitch

Working with two strands of embroidery thread in your needle, begin stitching in the centre of your fabric. You can stitch row by row, or complete each stitch before you move on to the next one – I tend to use the former method. Remember that when working on evenweave, you will make your stitches over two fabric threads each time (1).

For the first stitch bring the needle from the back to the front of the fabric. Leave a short tail of about 2.5cm (1in) at the back of the fabric and hold on to it. Stitch over it as you go on – this secures the thread and stops it coming undone.

Pass the needle back through the fabric at a position that is diagonally opposite where you came up, that is to say two fabric threads above and two fabric threads to the right.

Complete a whole row of these diagonal stitches, referring to the pattern to see how many of the colour you're using you need to stitch. Then work back in the opposite direction, working over two fabric threads, to complete the cross stitches (2). Make sure that your top stitches always slant in the same direction: if they don't it can make the finished stitching look messy.

Sometimes you will need to stitch individual stitches rather than rows, but the same method is used in working a single stitch.

Backstitch

Backstitch is used to add detail and outlines to a design and is usually done using one strand of thread. Work any backstitch on top of the cross stitches. You can leave it until the end, or do it as you complete an area of the design.

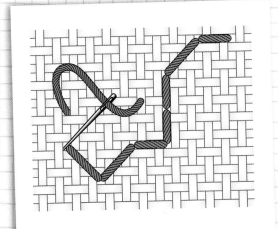

To begin, run the needle through the back of a few stitches on the reverse of your sewing, to secure the thread end. Push the needle through to the front of your work, where you want to start, then take the needle back down through the fabric to form a straight stitch, following the chart to see where to place your backstitch. Come back up one stitch length away from where the thread last passed through the fabric. Complete the stitch by passing the needle back through the same point at which the last stitch ended (see diagram). Some backstitch runs around the edges of the cross stitches and some runs over the top.

You can sew one backstitch for each square on the chart, or you can work it over two or three – it's up to you. I like to run it over a few squares, but be careful not to make your backstitches too long, as this can be messy and the stitches can lose definition.

To secure the thread, run the needle under a few stitches at the back of your stitching and snip any remaining thread. If you want to make any backstitch areas stand out more, you can sew with two strands of thread.

French Knots

Bring up your thread where you need the French knot on your stitching. Lay the needle flat against the fabric and hold it in place. Wrap the thread around the needle a few times – two or three times will do (1). Keeping the thread taut around the needle, pull the needle through and push it back through to the reverse side of the fabric, close to where the needle initially came up (2), then pull the thread tight. You should now have a small raised 'bobble' of thread, like a little dot on the front of your fabric (3).

You can increase or decrease the size of the French knot by adjusting the number of times that you wrap the thread around the needle. I find three wraps works well.

If you have more than one French knot, stitch the next one with the same thread – but don't jump too far across the back of your stitching as this can cause tension problems.

To secure, run the thread through a few stitches at the back of your sewing.

Stitch Counts and Design Sizes

For each doll I have indicated the size of fabric needed and the finished size of the doll. If you use 28-count evenweave fabric you will achieve the same results.

Following a Chart

The charts in this book are in colour, with black symbols on them – the symbols help to differentiate colours and are useful when some colours look similar to each other on the chart.

• Each square on the chart represents one stitch.

• Backstitch is indicated by a solid line on the chart, with the thread colours listed after the cross stitch colours in the key. Please note that different colours of backstitch are sometimes used in one design, so please pay attention to that, to achieve the desired results.

• French knots are indicated on the chart by a small dot. If you see them in the key, the design has French knots in it.

HOW TO MAKE UP THE DOLLS

Sew

Place the finished front and back pieces right sides together, being careful to match up the edges of the stitched design. Choose a section of the doll that has a straight edge of about 4-5cm (1½-2in) – the leg or edge of the skirt are ideal – this will be left unstitched for turning and stuffing.

Start sewing from your chosen point using a small freestyle backstitch, 2-3mm (1⁄16in) away from the edge of the design. This stitch is worked like the backstitch described in How to Cross Stitch, but you don't need to keep to the 'grid' of the fabric, just make your stitches neat and even, and follow the outline of the doll. It is important to open up the layers of fabric every few stitches to check that the front and back design edges remain aligned. Adjust as you go if needed.

You can use a few pins to hold the front and back together, but to get really neat results it is preferable to hold the pieces by hand so you can check regularly that everything is lined up.

Keep stitching all the way around the design, staying the same distance from the edge. Sew around the bottom of the feet without sewing up between the legs (where they are separate) and if the arms are close to the body, just sew around the hand rather than into a tight gap.

On tight corners sew generously away from the edges in a wide curve to allow easy turning and stuffing without puckering.

Finish stitching at the opposite end of the 4-5cm (1½-2in) gap and secure the thread.

Cut

Cut carefully around the design, leaving a 1cm (⅜in) seam allowance, apart from the opening which should have an allowance of at least 3cm (1⅛in).

Snip into the seam allowance at the points of any tight curves, such as under the arms, but don't go too close to the seam to avoid fraying.

Fill

Turn out the doll to the right side through the opening and use a chopstick to push out any corners, including the arms and legs.

Fill the doll starting at the head, using small pieces of toy stuffing at a time, and pushing them into place with a finger or chopstick. Once the doll is gently rounded, but not too firm, fold the seam allowance fabric back inside the doll and close the gap with ladder stitch.

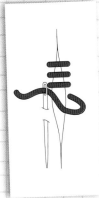

To work ladder stitch, first make a knot in your thread and then insert your needle from inside the doll through the fold of the seam allowance at one end of the stuffing opening. Make a straight stitch across the gap, then make a tiny stitch parallel to the opening, within the fold of the seam allowance, before making another straight stitch across the gap in the other direction. The stitches across the gap look like the rungs of a ladder. Pull the thread to draw the edges of the opening together, then continue to make small tidy stitches in the same way until the gap is closed. To finish, leave a loop in the last stitch and pass your needle through it before pulling tight.

Finish

Using white cotton, backstitch along the gap between the legs and under the arms (depending on the design), taking care to go through both layers of fabric and the stuffing.

ABOUT THE AUTHOR

Susan studied a Fine Art degree, with the focus on painting. After finishing her studies she worked in a shop in London which sold hand-painted needlepoint designs. Her love of painting and the needlepoint designs Susan saw in the shop inspired her to produce her own needlepoint creations.

Her early designs were sold to a publishing company that produced a part-work sewing magazine. Alongside the needlepoint designs, she was asked to start making cross stitch patterns for them too.

Cross stitch became Susan's main focus in her freelance design career, a passion she has carried with her throughout her career.

Now an experienced cross stitch designer, Susan has had her work featured in many cross stitch magazines. She is a regular contributor to *Cross Stitcher* and *The World of Cross Stitching*. Her reputation was further enhanced in Europe with her designs being included in the Turkish magazine *Kanaviçe*. In addition to this she has produced a number of cross stitch books.

Herrschners (an American company) prints her design work and also makes kits from them. She designs on a regular basis for the U.S. company Stitchable Cards, producing patterns for their subscription kits and starring in their live-stream 'how to' YouTube broadcasts. Susan has also designed for DMC and has had her designs made into kits by them.

She teaches knitting and crochet to beginners at her home in East Sussex. In her spare time Susan enjoys designing and making her own clothes.

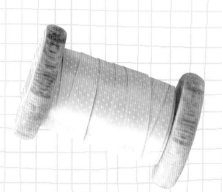

Acknowledgements

Firstly I'd like to thank Ame Verso for giving me the opportunity to work on this book. Thanks also to the rest of the team at David and Charles who worked on this project. They are: Anna Wade (head of design), Prudence Rogers (book design and art direction), Jane Trollope and Victoria Allen (book editors) and Jason Jenkins (photography). My thanks go to the stitchers: Madeleine Ayme-McLean, Eleanor Cooper, Sandra Doolan, Nicola Gravener, Caroline Grayling, Emma Rhodes.

I'd also like to say a big thank you to James Stanger and my family. They have always supported me and encouraged me in my design work, even when I'm stressing and worrying about deadlines and work schedules! Thanks too go to my mum, whose love of sewing has been a big influence on me.

INDEX

A DAVID AND CHARLES BOOK
© David and Charles, Ltd 2024

David and Charles is an imprint of David and Charles, Ltd
Suite A, Tourism House, Pynes Hill, Exeter, EX2 5WS

Text and Designs © Susan Bates 2024
Layout and Photography © David and Charles, Ltd 2024

First published in the UK and USA in 2024

A catalogue record for this book is available from the British Library.

ISBN-13: 9781446310151 paperback
ISBN-13: 9781446310168 EPUB
ISBN-13: 9781446310243 PDF

This book has been printed on paper from approved suppliers and made from pulp from sustainable sources.

Printed in China through Asia Pacific Offset for:
David and Charles, Ltd
Suite A, Tourism House, Pynes Hill, Exeter, EX2 5WS

10 9 8 7 6 5 4 3 2 1

Publishing Director: Ame Verso
Managing Editor: Jeni Chown
Editor: Victoria Allen
Project Editor: Jane Trollope
Head of Design: Anna Wade
Pre-press Designer: Susan Reansbury
Illustrations: Kuo Kang Chen
Design and Art Direction: Prudence Rogers
Photography: Jason Jenkins
Production Manager: Beverley Richardson

David and Charles publishes high-quality books on a wide range of subjects. For more information visit www.davidandcharles.com.

Share your makes with us on social media using #dandcbooks and follow us on Facebook and Instagram by searching for @dandcbooks.

Layout of the digital edition of this book may vary depending on reader hardware and display settings.